A Proposal Writing Manual for Graduate and Post-graduate Students

Dr. Mitra Farsi
Dr. Seyyed Ali Kazemi
Dr. Mohammad S. Bagheri

دانشیار

PREFACE

Graduate students are required to conduct independent, individual research in the academic field of their chosen master program. They should also write some papers and articles before graduation. Students should be able to report the entire research process leading to the master thesis, from problem formulation to describing findings, conclusions and recommendations. The aim of the master thesis is to provide master students with insights, experiences and tips for improving their skills in research. It forms an integral and important part of all programs. This manual gives detailed requirements for the structure, content and assessment of the master thesis.

This manual is specifically written for graduate and post-graduate students with little or no experience in writing proposals, papers and articles. However, no matter what your experience level, this manual helps you get better at writing proposals, papers and articles. Different disciplines may have different expectations and requirements on the substance, format and length of a proposal. In this regard, students are strongly advised to consult their supervisor(s) and the department beforehand.

We welcome the oral and written comments and reflections with open arms.

Board of Editors

CONTENTS

CHAPTER ONE
WHAT IS A PROPOSAL?

1.1 What is a thesis proposal?

The thesis proposal is a statement that summarizes the research project you intend to perform and include in your thesis. A research project addresses a research problem. This problem is framed as a research question for which the thesis will offer an answer or solution.

1.2 Parts of a Thesis or Dissertation

Proposals across programs generally have some form of the following sections. You can check with your academic advisors about the specific sections they require. The following is the standard order of components of either an electronic thesis or dissertation. The components will be explained below.

Preliminary Pages

Title page (required; do not number this page)

Dedication page (optional)

List of abbreviations or symbols (required when symbols are not self-explanatory)

Acknowledgments (optional)

Table of contents (required; number this page, but do not list among the contents)

List of tables (required when tables are used)

List of figures or illustrations (required when figures are used)

Abstract *(required; number this page ii) - must not exceed 250 words*

Body of Manuscript

References

Appendices

1.3 Importance of writing a strong thesis proposal

Clear research problem (or question) is essential to the success of a study. If you spend time on describing your project in your proposal, you can write your thesis faster and more easily because you can solidify key elements. Also, your proposal can function as a guide to help you stay on track while writing your thesis.

1.4 Title

Before getting started, you should provide a working title. You'd better look at your variables and decide on the exact wording for your title when you are about to complete your proposal. Generally, a title beginning "A study in ..." is unclear; you should say whether you want to compare, collate, assess, etc. A good title should orient readers to the topic that you are going to research. It should also indicate the type of study that you are going to conduct.

Example:
Teaching English as a Second Language to Children and Adults: Variations in Practices
The title should:
1. Offer major variables or theoretical issues under investigation
2. Be specific and to the point
3. Must have a maximum of 12 words
4. Must avoid the following phrases to prevent superfluity or redundancy: e. g "A study of", "An Analysis of", "A Correlation of" and "an investigation of".

1.5 Title Page

The title page should follow the prescribed content, as listed immediately below, of the school. The title page must also follow the prescribed format as illustrated in the sample title page offered.

1.5.1 A sample title page

In the Name of God

Islamic Azad University

Xxxxxx Branch

M.A. Thesis Proposal in English Language Teaching

Subject

Construct Validation of Analytic Rating Scales in a Speaking Assessment

Thesis Advisor
Xxxx xxxx, PhD

Consulting advisor
Xxxxx xxxxx, PhD

1.6 Acknowledgement Page

In the acknowledgement page, the candidate may express his or her gratitude to individuals or institutions helping or supporting the candidate in the conduct of the research.

1.6.1 Sample Acknowledgement Page

Acknowledgements

I would like to thank xxxx for coding part of the data, xxx for statistical advice, and xxxx and the three anonymous reviewers of *Language Testing* for their valuable comments. I am also indebted to xxx, who gave me permission to use the cloze test used in xxx *et al.* (1989), and to Prentice Hall which gave me permission to use xxx. Needless to say, the positions taken and any errors that may remain are solely my responsibility. The research reported in the present paper was funded by a research grant for the 1995 academic year from xxxx University.

1.7 Abstract of the Study

For the abstract of the study, this must contain the general problem, Methodology, major findings and conclusions. Ideally, it should not exceed 250 words.

1.8 Writing an Abstract

The word abstract comes from the Latin abstractum, which means a condensed form of a longer piece of writing. There are two main types of abstract: the (1) Descriptive and the (2) Informative abstract. The type of abstract you write depends on your discipline area. The abstract is the last item that you write, but the first thing people read when they want to have a quick overview of the whole paper. We suggest you leave writing the abstract to the end, because you will have a clearer picture of all your findings and conclusions.

1.8.1 Steps in writing an abstract

- First re-read your paper/report for an overview. Then read each section and shrink the information in each down to 1-2 sentences;
- Next read these sentences again to ensure that they cover the major points in your paper;
- Ensure you have written something for each of the key points outlined above for either the descriptive or informative abstract;
- Check the word length and further reduce your words if necessary by cutting out unnecessary words or rewriting some of the sentences into a single, more succinct sentence; and
- Edit for flow and expression.

A good abstract does the following:

- Uses one well-developed paragraph that is coherent and concise, and is able to stand alone as a unit of information; Covers all the essential academic elements of the full-length paper, namely the background, purpose, focus, methods, results and conclusions;
- Contains no information not included in the paper;
- Is written in plain English and is understandable to a wider audience, as well as to your discipline-specific audience;
- Often uses passive structures in order to report on findings, focusing on the issues rather than people;
- Uses the language of the original paper, often in a more simplified form for the more general reader;
- Usually does not include any referencing; and

- In publications such as journals, it is found at the beginning of the text, but in academic assignments, it is placed on a separate preliminary page.

1.8.2 Types of abstracts

1. Descriptive abstracts are generally used for humanities and social science papers or psychology essays. This type of abstract is usually very short (50-100 words). Most descriptive abstracts have certain key parts in common. They are:

- Background
- Purpose
- Particular interest/focus of paper
- Overview of contents (not always included)

2. Informative abstracts are generally used for science, engineering or psychology reports. You must get the essence of what your report is about, usually in about 150-250 words. Most informative abstracts also have key parts in common. Each of these parts might consist of 1-2 sentences. The parts include:

- Background
- Aim or purpose of research
- Method used
- Findings/results
- Conclusion

In both types of abstract, your advisor or supervisor may require other specific information to be included. Always follow your advisor or supervisor's instructions and advice.

1.8.3 A sample abstract

A Critical Examination of ELT in Thailand: The Role of Cultural Awareness
Will Baker
Southampton University United Kingdom

Abstract ■ With the increasingly significant role that English language teaching (ELT) is playing in Asian contexts, it is important to gain a better understanding of the use of English as a medium of intercultural communication in Asia. In doing so, ELT practices may be better able to adapt themselves to the intercultural communicative needs of local contexts. This paper argues that an essential element in fostering successful intercultural communication is developing cultural awareness as part of ELT pedagogy. To illustrate this, a case study of Thailand is presented examining English use, English teaching policy and practice, and local cultural attitudes towards ELT. This then leads to suggestions on how locally relevant intercultural communicative practices can form part of ELT classroom pedagogy in Thailand with the aim of developing learners' cultural awareness. It is argued that similar analyses may be applied to other Asian contexts, which may share features with the Thai context. This can lead to the development of teaching practices, which through engaging learners in intercultural reflection will result in English language users who are better able to manage intercultural communication through English.

Keywords ■ cultural awareness, ELT, intercultural communication, Thailand.

1.9 Table of Contents

The table of contents must contain the main section and subsections of thesis or dissertation (in order which they are presented) and the corresponding page where the section or subsection starts. A sample is shown here.

1.9.1 A Table of Contents Sample (A completed Thesis)

Table of Contents

1.10 List of Tables and Figures

The numbering of the tables and figures should follow the order in which they are presented in the text.

Examples of a list of tables and figures are shown below.

1.10.1 A list of tables sample

List of Tables

1.10.2 A list of figures sample
List of Figures

CHAPTER TWO
MAJOR CHAPTERS OF A THESIS

2.1 The five major chapters of a thesis (Body of Manuscript):   The five major chapters of a thesis are: the introduction, review of related literature, design and methodology, Results/findings and discussion, and conclusion.

2.1.1Chapter 1: The Introduction

The Introduction is not a narrative. It is only a heading under which the following five narrative sections appear: General Statement of the Problem, Significance of the Thesis, Research Question(s), Assumptions, and Definitions of Terms. These sections help the reader understand what will be presented in the thesis, and why.

2.1.2 Chapter 2: Review of Related Literature

This section outlines what you learned from previous contributors to the field. It makes the researcher(s) and the reader(s) up to date on what others have done relevant to the topic. The Review of Related Literature section addresses the questions "How unique is this thesis?" "Is it a logical expansion of previous work?" and "Has this already been done?" / "What is the novelty of research?"

2.1.3 Chapter 3: Design and Methodology

This is not a narrative, but a heading under which the sections on Subjects, Instrumentation/Data Collection, and Data Treatment/Procedures appear.

The method section is to provide sufficient detail about your experiment to enable readers to evaluate its appropriateness or to replicate your study should they desire to do so. This section helps readers to determine the validity of the research. Can the data collected, for example, actually be used to answer the question being asked?

2.1.4 Chapter 4: Results/ Findings and discussion

This is an important thesis section, with narrative and other material attached. It includes your actual findings. Report and discuss your results here. Use charts, tables, and graphs when appropriate, but include a narrative that describes what you consider the most relevant information. Try to make each tabular display appear on a single page, so readers can see it at a glance. Present as many summary displays as appropriate, so that you will not have to discuss every detail. Be sure to include potential implications, as well as the facts. Explain carefully how your Findings confirm or diverge from those of previous researchers.

2.1.5 Chapter 5: Conclusion

Limit this section to a discussion of summarized data that were presented earlier in your thesis. Do not present new information. Use the Conclusion to articulate your main points with clarity; to reiterate, summarize, and perhaps re-sequence the Findings; and to start winding down your thesis narrative. This sections also includes Recommendations for Further Research, and limitations of the study.

2.2 Chapter one in detail:
2.2.1 Introduction/Background

Basically, the introduction provides essential background information to your study and provides your readers with your overall research interest. An ideal introduction should:

- Set up the general territory in which the study is placed.
- Describe the broad basis of your study, including some references to existing literature and/or empirically observable situations. Put differently, the introduction should provide sufficient background for readers to understand where your study is coming from.
- Present the general scope of your study, but do not go into so much detail that later sections (purpose/literature review) become irrelevant.
- Gives an overview of the sections that are going to appear in your proposal.

2.2.2 Purpose/Aims/Rationale/Research Questions

Most proposals have a clear statement of the research objectives, including a description of the questions the research is going to answer or the hypotheses the research advances. This can be included as part of the introduction, or it may be a separate section. Allocate enough time brainstorming when you draft this section. When you start your thesis research, your aims may change in emphasis or in number. The essential point is to specify for your readers the precise focus of your research and to identify key concepts that you are going to study.

A good statement of purpose should:
- Explain the goals and objectives of the study.
- Show the originality and new contributions of your study by explaining how your research questions or approach are different from previous research.
- Provide a more detailed account of the points summarized in the introduction.
- Incorporate a rationale for the study (The reason why we should study this?).
- Be clear about what your study is not going to address.

This section may also:
- Describe your research questions and/or hypotheses.
- Include a subsection defining important terms, especially if they will be new to some readers.
- State limitations of your study.
- Give a rationale for the particular subjects of your study.

Generally, Chapter 1 contains five sections in the following order. Introduction, Historical and Contextual Backgrounds of the Problem, Statement of the Problem, Significance of the Study, Scope and Limitations & Delimitations.

2.2.3 Historical and Contextual Backgrounds of the Problem
This section contains a state of the art review of the field of study, including past and current developments, controversies and breakthroughs, previous research and relevant background theory of the research topic. More importantly, it answers the questions: What is the gap between existing bodies of knowledge and the prevailing subject situation that needs to be filled? What is the problem that needs to be solved?

2.2.4 Statement of the Problem: There are two parts, the general problem and the specific problems. The general problem should be stated in declarative form. The main problem should be-consistent with the title of the study. On the other hand, the specific problem which is a breakdown of the general problem, is either in question form or in declarative form. The questions must be clearly and logically presented and be connected to the title of the thesis or dissertation.

2.2.5 Significance of the Study: This section identifies who will benefit from the results of the study, such as specific institutions or groups of individuals or the researcher himself or herself will be benefited. It answers the questions: Why is the study important? To whom is it important? What benefit(s) will occur for each of them if the study is done?

2.2.5 Scope and Limitations: This section defines the coverage and sets the limitation or boundaries of the research to provide a clear focus involving the following aspects of the study and briefly explains the following: rationale behind each limitation or exclusion beyond which the study is not concerned. It discusses its nature, its coverage and its timeframe. It also briefly explains its subject matter, its geographic locale, and its duration as well as the rationale behind the limits of the study. It indicates the variables that should have been included in the study, cites the reasons for their exclusion and how this is expected to affect the results of the study.

2.2.7 Research Paradigm: This section expounds on the concepts, variables and its indicators that led to the formulation of the research problem and its corresponding hypothesis. These concepts, constructs and variables should be presented in a framework. Examples of these are the input-process-output-feedback paradigm or the independent-moderating- dependent variable paradigm.

2.2.8 Research Hypothesis: The hypothesis is what the study would like to test. It is a predictive statement that relates an independent variable to a dependent variable. Usually, a research hypothesis must contain, at least, one independent and one Dependent variable, This is presented in its null form.

Examples:
H0: **There are** no significant differences among the depositors' assessments on the select strategies/ practices adopted by banks operating in the Philippines to foster confidence in the banking system.

H0: **There are** no significant differences between BSP and PDIC's assessments with regard to the select strategies/ practices adopted by banks operating in the Philippines to foster confidence in the banking system.

Not all researches, however, require a hypothesis. For example, qualitative research does not necessarily test **hypothesis/es**. But quantitative research requires hypothesis/es.

2.2.9 Operational Definition of Variables: The researcher should clearly and concisely define the variables found in the research paradigm. What is needed here is not necessarily the conceptual definition or how they are defined in dictionaries but rather the operational or functional definition, i.e., the specific way the variables are used in the study. The list of the variables should be alphabetized.

Examples:
Active Deposit- an account that has shown activity, either by increase through deposits or decrease through withdrawals within a period of two (2) years.

This section does not appear in qualitative research where there are no variables of the study, unless a combination of both quantitative and qualitative approaches are used.

2.3 Review of Related Literature
2.3.1 Introduction
The literature review provides critical look at the existing research that is significant to the work that you are going to conduct. Clearly, at this point you are not likely to have read everything related to your research questions, but you should be able to identify the key texts with which you will be in conversation as you conduct your study. Literature reviews generally include both the theoretical approaches to your topic and research (empirical or analytical) on your topic.

2.3.2 Literature Review
A literature review is a description of the literature relevant to a particular field or topic. This is often written as part of a postgraduate thesis proposal, or at the commencement of a thesis. A critical literature review is a critical assessment of the relevant literature. It is unlikely that you will be able to write a truly critical assessment of the literature until you have a good grasp of the subject, usually at some point near the end of your thesis.

2.3.2.1 What counts as 'literature'?
"Literature" covers everything "*relevant*" that is written on a topic: books, journal articles, newspaper articles, historical records, government reports, theses, dissertations, etc.

A literature review gives an overview of the field of inquiry: what has already been said on the topic, who the key writers are, what the prevailing theories and hypotheses are, what questions are being asked, and what methodologies and methods are appropriate and useful. A critical literature review shows how prevailing ideas fit into your own thesis, and how your thesis agrees or differs from them.

2.3.2.2 How to Write A Literature Review
- Find out what has been written on your subject. Use as many bibliographical sources as you can to find relevant titles.

Write down the full bibliographical details of each book or article as soon as you find a reference to it. This will save you an enormous amount of time later on.

- Once you have what looks like a list of relevant texts, you have to find them.

The full text of many journal articles can be found on electronic databases.

- Read the literature and take notes. You are reading to find out how each piece of writing approaches the subject of your research, what it has to say about it, and (especially for research students) how it relates to your own thesis:

  Usually, you won't have to read the whole text from the first to the last page. Learn to use efficient scanning and skimming reading techniques.

- Having gathered the relevant details about the literature, you now need to write the review. The kind of review you write, and the amount of detail, will depend on the level of your studies.

Important note: *do not confuse a literature review with an annotated bibliography*.

An *annotated bibliography* deals with each text in turn, describing and evaluating the text, using one paragraph for each text.

In contrast, a *literature review* synthesizes many texts in one paragraph. Each paragraph (or section if it is a long thesis) of the literature review should classify and evaluate the themes of the texts that are relevant to your thesis; each paragraph or section of your review should deal with a different aspect of the literature.

- Like all academic writing, a literature review must have an introduction, body, and conclusion.

The **introduction** of a literature review should include:
- the nature of the topic under discussion (the topic of your thesis)
- the parameters of the topic (what does it include and exclude?)

The **conclusion** of a literature review should include:
- A summary of major agreements and disagreements in the literature
- A summary of general conclusions that are being drawn
- A summary of where your thesis sits in the literature
  The **body** paragraphs in a literature review could include relevant paragraphs on:
- historical background
- current mainstream versus alternative theoretical or ideological viewpoints
- definitions in use
- current research studies
- current discoveries about the topic
- principal questions that are being asked
- general conclusions that are being drawn

- methodologies and methods in use

Theory Guiding the Study/ Theoretical Framework: This section discusses the existing theory or body of theories that serves as the core support of the research. Well – known authority sources to support the theory or theories are cited.

Related Literature and studies: Possible sources of literature are books, journals, published and unpublished studies, monographs, and other scholarly publications. The main idea or ideas from each source should be clearly and concisely presented.

One way of presenting this section is to present local and foreign literature separately, with local literature presented first. Another format is to present the literature by topic. Unless the literature is a classic, it is strongly suggested that more recent literature, at least in the last 10 years, are cited. Literature review must be outlined and theme-based.

2.4 Methodology

This section is essential to most good research proposals. The way that you study a problem is often as important as the results you collect. This section contains a description of the general means through which the goals of the study will be achieved: methods, participants, materials, procedures, tasks, etc.

A. Participants: Report information regarding participants here. Mention:
number of participants, demographic characteristics: gender (number or % of each), ethnicity (African American, Asian Pacific Islander, Native American, Hispanic and/or Latino, Caucasian, and other), age range, average age, Socioeconomic Status, Level of Education, Class rank if college students are used.

Also, describe where they are from, how they are selected, how they are assigned to groups (if applicable), and what incentives for participation they have, if any(e.g., payment or course credit).

If they have important characteristics, describe them, e.g., depressed, determined and if participants are excluded, explain why and describe the criteria for inclusion/exclusion in the study. Also, report final sample size. e.g. "Two participants were excluded from the study. The remaining sample consisted of …. participants."

B. Materials (Measures / Apparatus)

If you are using paper pencil tests (questionnaires) or their computer equivalents each one used should be described in detail and include examples of items, a description of how measures were computed from the questionnaires, the mean, the standard deviation, and the range. Also, for scales with multiple items, the Cronbach's

Alpha should be reported.

C. Procedure

1. Include a complete description of what happened to the participants, in chronological order, fromA-Z.
2. Include the description of the design (experimental, quasi-experimental, longitudinal, etc).
3. Provide an operational definition of the questionnaires and their validity and reliability coefficients.
4. Provide information on how the questionnaires are scored.

D. Data Analysis

Give the reader a roadmap to the analyses you plan to conduct. This is especially important if you are conducting very complicated analyses that the average reader may not be familiar with.

E. Research design

The final chapter of the research proposal, chapter three, also begins with an introductory paragraph which states the research design to be used (which may be quantitative and/ or qualitative in data- collection and analysis) as well as the objective of the chapter.

This chapter should include five sections in the following order. Research Locale, Sources of Data and Sample, Instrument for Gathering Data and Validation, Procedure for Gathering Data, and Statistics for Analyzing Data.

Research Locale **(area or place).** This section contains a description of where the data was gathered. It may be a geographical unit, an organization or the population from where the sample was drawn. The description may include basic facts such as total population, mean age of the population, mean income, or some other important demographic variables which shall serve as independed variables.

Sources of Data and Sample: This section has two parts: the first part contains a discussion of data employed and libraries tapped. The type of data used whether primary (from the original source) or secondary (from published sources) is also mentioned. Furthermore, information from the abovementioned data sources that are used or needed in the study should be mentioned.

The second part describes the sample profile which shall serve as independent variables, sample size based on the researcher's desired confidence level and desired margin- of-error from the true mean of the dependent variable based on the measurement scale used to measure the latter and sampling procedure that was used in the research. The sampling techniques often used are probability sampling(simple random sampling, stratified, cluster and systematic sampling) or non- probability sampling(improvised, convenience or quota sampling).

2.5 Sampling

Quantitative researchers typically use probability samples that allow them to generalize their findings to a large population. Probability samples are constructed by ensuring that every possible combination of elements of a given size has an equal probability of being the selected sample. Since they are based on probability, probability samples allow researchers to use statistics calculated from the sample to draw conclusions about the larger population.

I. Probability sampling.

Probability samples are based on random selection in which every element in the population has an equal probability of being selected for the sample.

Types of probability samples

1. **Simple random samples:** In a simple random sample, a list of every element in the population is obtained or produced (the list is called a sampling frame) and elements are randomly selected ensuring that each element on the list has an equal chance of being chosen. Choosing probability sampling may require:
- Populations and sampling frames.
- Using random number tables to select elements.
- Using computers to randomly select elements.

2. **Systematic random sample.**
a. In a systematic random sample, a list of every element in the population is obtained or produced and elements are randomly selected by randomly selecting a starting point, then skipping a pre-determined number of cases (the sampling interval) to select the next case, and so on. Other essential points are:
- Determining a starting point using a random number table or computer generated random number.
- Calculating the sampling interval.

3. **Stratified random sample.**
a. In stratified random samples, the sampling frame is divided (or stratified) along selected criteria (such as race, age, and gender) then elements are selected from the stratified lists using either simple random or systematic random sampling. The goal is to ensure proportional representation of the selected criteria. This sampling has 3 stages:
- Stratifying the sampling frame.

- Selecting cases using simple random or systematic <u>random sampling</u>.
- Over-sampling and weighting.

4. Multistage cluster designs

Unlike the three sampling designs discussed above, multistage cluster designs do not require that a sampling frame list every element in the population of interest be produced or obtained up front. Rather, it samples naturally occurring groups elements (you will need a list of the groups), sometimes at multiple levels, and then it samples elements from within these groups.

Identifying and sampling naturally occurring groupings requires:

i.   Using multiple levels of naturally occurring groups.
i.   Obtaining or producing sampling frames.
ii. Sampling groups and elements.
iii. Probability proportionate to size adjustments.

II. Non-probability sampling.

Qualitative researchers are not generally concerned about statistical inference or hypothesis testing. Therefore, they typically use non-probability techniques. While quantitative researches tend to use probability sampling whenever possible, in some instances it is difficult, if not impossible, to do probability sampling. In these instances, non-probability techniques may be used. Non-probability sampling may be used because the sample is small or difficult to identify populations due to limited time and resources.

Types of non-probability samples
1. Convenience samples.
2. Quota samples.
3. Snowball samples.
4. Self-selected samples.
5. Purposive or theoretical samples.

2.5.1 Doing sampling in quantitative research
A. Define your population and, if possible, obtain a sampling frame.
B. Choose a sampling technique.
Consider your population and the availability of a sampling frame. Also, consider feasibility and cost. Use probability sampling if at all possible.

C. Determine sample size. Take into account the following:
- Factors affecting sample size.
- Size and variability in the population.
- Degree of accuracy desired.
- Number of variables and type of analyses to be performed.

- Expected return rate.
- Calculating sample size.

General rules for determining sample size

- For populations under 1,000, sample 30%.
- For populations around 10,000 sample 10%.
- For populations over 100,000, sample 1.5%.
- For populations over 1,000,000, sample .2%.
- For populations over 10,000,000 sample .025%.
- Large populations require smaller sampling ratios, not smaller samples.
- Samples of 2500 have been shown to be adequate for even the largest of populations.

D. Draw your sample.

2.5.2 Doing sampling in qualitative research

- Identify possible cases.
- Determine how many cases will be needed.
- Consider the goals of the research.
- Consider your sensitizing concepts and questions.
- Consider availability, time, and cost.
- Consider which case or cases are likely to provide the most relevant data.
- Select your case or cases, most likely using non-probability techniques.

Nonrandom Sampling Techniques

The other major type of sampling used in quantitative research is nonrandom sampling (i.e., when you do not use one of the ransom sampling techniques). There are four main types of nonrandom sampling:

- The first type of nonrandom sampling is called *convenience sampling* (i.e., it simply involves using the people who are the most available or the most easily selected to be in your research study).

- The second type of nonrandom sampling is called *quota sampling* (i.e., it involves setting quotas and then using convenience sampling to obtain those quotas). A set of quotas might be given to you as follows: find 25 African American males, 25 European American males, 25 African American females, and 25 European American females. You use convenience sampling to actually find the people, but you must make sure you have the right number of people for each quota.

- The third type of nonrandom sampling is called *purposive sampling* (i.e., the researcher specifies the characteristics of the population of interest and then locates individuals who match those characteristics). For example, you might decide that you want to only include "boys who are in the 7th grade and have been diagnosed with ADHD" in your research study. You would then, try to find 50 students who meet your "inclusion criteria" and include them in your research study.

- The fourth type of nonrandom sampling is called *snowball sampling* (i.e., each research participant is asked to identify other potential research participants who have a certain characteristic). You start with one or a few participants, ask them for more, find those, ask them for some, and continue until you have a sufficient sample size. This technique might be used for a hard to find population (e.g., where no sampling frame exists). For example, you might want to use snowball sampling if you wanted to do a study of people in your city who have a lot of power in the area of educational policy making (in addition to the already known positions of power, such as the school board and the school system superintendent).

You will need *larger* samples under these circumstances:

- When the population is very *heterogeneous*.
- When you want to breakdown the data into multiple categories.
- When you want a relatively *narrow confidence interval*.
- When you expect a *weak relationship* or a *small effect*.
- When you use a *less efficient technique* of random sampling (e.g., cluster sampling is less efficient than proportional stratified sampling).
- When you expect to have *a low response rate*. The response rate is the percentage of people in your sample who agree to be in your study.

Instrument for Gathering Data and Validation. If a survey is employed, a research instrument could be in the form of questionnaire or an interview schedule, observation guide or other documents used in gathering data to answer the statement of the problem. Specific parts of the research instrument are discussed in this section.

Samples of these instruments should be presented in the appendices. In the case of a questionnaire, include a cover letter that should introduce the confidentiality of the researcher, state the title and objectives of the research. Emphasize the confidentiality of the research, as well as a request for the cooperation of the respondent in completing the survey instrument.

If immersion in the real- life setting were used to answer the statement of the problem in pure Qualitative Research, the research instrument would be the observation guide with the use of either a diary, or a logbook, or a journal for noting down observed behavior or gathering data from participants.

All instruments to be used or used in the research should be described in detail.

Procedure for Gathering Data. This section discusses in full detail the procedures to be followed in conducting the study. It describes the techniques, devices and Procedures in gathering data. **Present in a flow chart the Procedure in the study with a concise description of each step in paragraph form.**
In case of experiments, this section should include instruction given to participants, the experimental manipulations, the control features in the design, the formation of groups as to the random assignment from the population that were assigned- one for the control group and the other for the experimental group.

Statistics for Analyzing Data. This section will discuss the statistical techniques and formulas that will be used in the study and their rationale.

2.6 Results and Discussion

This chapter should begin with an introductory paragraph showing the contents and purpose of the chapter and a concluding paragraph to re-cap this chapter as well as introduce the next chapter.

This chapter contains all of the results, but no conclusions.

Order of the results: first, Descriptive statistics, then, Tests with Demographic Variables, and after that Inferential statistics.

Tell the reader what variables were tested and which analyses were significant, if any. For example: No Significant Associations were found. Data gathered are presented in this chapter in the form of tables, graphs and statistical results.

The presentation should follow the ordering of the specific questions raised. Major captions for each question answered should use bold font.

2.6.1 Discussion

This section contains the conclusions that can be drawn from the results of your data analysis. The purpose of the Discussion is to state your interpretations and opinions, explain the implications of your findings, and make suggestions for future research. Its main function is to answer the questions posed in the Introduction, explain how the results support the answers and, how the answers fit in with existing knowledge on the topic (literature).

To make your message clear, the discussion should be kept as short as possible while clearly and fully stating, supporting, explaining, and defending your answers and discussing other important and directly relevant issues. Care must be taken to provide a commentary and not a reiteration of the results. Side issues should not be included, as these tend to obscure the message.

The Discussion is considered the heart of the paper and usually requires several writing attempts.

' 2.6.1.1 Fourteen Steps to Writing an Effective Discussion Section

1. Organize the Discussion from the specific to the general: your findings to the literature, to theory, to practice.

2. Use the same key terms, the same verb tense (present tense), and the same point of view that you used when posing the questions in the Introduction.

3. Begin by re-stating the hypothesis you were testing and answering the questions posed in the introduction.

4. Support the answers with the results. Explain how your results relate to expectations and to the literature, clearly stating why they are acceptable and how they are consistent or fit in with previously published knowledge on the topic.

5. Address all the results relating to the questions, regardless of whether or not the findings were statistically significant.

6. Describe the patterns, principles, and relationships shown by each major finding/result and put them in perspective. The sequencing of providing this information is important; first state the answer, then the relevant results, then cite the work of others. If necessary, point the reader to a figure or table to enhance the "story".

7. Defend your answers, if necessary, by explaining both why your answer is satisfactory and why others are not. Only by giving both sides to the argument can you make your explanation convincing.

8. Discuss and evaluate conflicting explanations of the results. This is the sign of a good discussion.

9. Discuss any unexpected findings. When discussing an unexpected finding, begin the paragraph with the finding and then describe it.

10. Identify potential limitations and weaknesses and comment on the relative importance of these to your interpretation of the results and how they may affect the validity of the findings. When identifying limitations and weaknesses, avoid using an apologetic tone.

11. Summarize concisely the principal implications of the findings, regardless of statistical significance.

12. Provide recommendations (no more than two) for further research. Do not offer suggestions which could have been easily addressed within the study, as this shows there has been inadequate examination and interpretation of the data.

13. Explain how the results and conclusions of this study are important and how they influence our knowledge or understanding of the problem being examined.

14. In your writing of the Discussion, discuss everything, but be concise, brief, and specific.

2.6.2 Summary

The final chapter should likewise include an introductory paragraph that shows the contents of the Chapter and a concluding paragraph. The key findings, conclusions and recommendations are presented in this chapter. The key findings must follow the logical sequence of the statement of the problem, while the conclusions must focus on the results of hypothesis testing. New ideas, tables or figures must be excluded in this section of the manuscript.

2.6.3 Conclusion

Combine the Interpretations in the Statistical description and/or Statistical analysis and Interpretation in Chapter 4.

2.6.3.1 Writing a Conclusion

The purpose of a conclusion is to tie together, or integrate the various issues, research, etc., covered in the body of the paper, and to make comments upon the meaning of all of it. This includes noting any implications resulting from your discussion of the topic, as well as recommendations, forecasting future trends, and the need for further research.

The conclusion should:

- be a logical ending to what has previously been discussed. It must pull together all of the parts of your argument and refer the reader back to the focus you have outlined in your introduction and to the central topic. This gives your essay a sense of unity.
- never contain any new information.
- usually be only a paragraph in length, but in an extended essay (3000+ words) it may be better to have two or three paragraphs to pull together the different parts of the essay.
- add to the overall quality and impact of the essay. This is your final statement about this topic; thus it can make a great impact on the reader.

The conclusion should not:

- just sum up
- end with a long quotation
- focus merely on a minor point in your argument
- introduce new material

The content of a conclusion may include:

- a summary of the arguments presented in the body and how these relate to the essay questions
- a restatement of the main point of view presented in the introduction in response to the topic
- the implications of this view or what might happen as a result

2.6.3.2 Steps in writing the conclusion

Begin with a sentence that refers to the main subject that was discussed in the body in the essay. Make sure that this sentence also links to the preceding paragraph, or uses phrase such as In conclusion to signal that these are your final words on the subject.

Then, you may give a brief summary of your argument and identify the main reasons/causes/factors that relate to the question you have been asked to address. Summarize concisely the principal implications of the findings, regardless of statistical significance.

Finally, it is a good idea to add a sentence or two to reinforce the thesis statement which was used in your introduction. This shows the reader that you have done what you said you would do and gives a sense of unity the essay. Explain how the results and conclusions of this study are important and how they influence our knowledge or understanding of the problem being examined.

Provide recommendations for further research. Generally, although a short pithy quote can sometimes be used to spice up your conclusion, the conclusion should be in your own words. Try to avoid direct quotations, or references to other sources.

Discussion

After the portrayal of the arguments and results of the research, we go to the **Discussion.** The questions asked in the problem formulation are answered here. If you posed hypotheses, here, present whether the research results confirm or refute these. Besides, you may answer the following questions:

- How generalizable are your results to other cases than those researched?
- How do the research results relate to the findings and conclusions of other authors?
- What has your study added to the knowledge about the topic at hand?
- What future line of research does your study open?

On the basis of the aim of your study, answering the following questions may also be valuable:

- What does your study say about the adequacy of the methods followed and the materials chosen? How could future researchers do a better job?
- Which recommendations can be made based on your study?
- Which predictions can be made on based on your study?

Conclusion

The conclusion of a research thesis reaffirms the thesis statement, discusses the issues, and reaches a final judgment. The conclusion is not just a summary; it is a belief based on your reasoning and on the evidence you have accumulated as recommendations, forecasting future trends, and the need for further research. The conclusion chapter or section seeks to:

1. tie together, integrate and synthesize the various issues raised in the

discussion sections, whilst reflecting the introductory thesis statement or objectives

2. provide answers to the thesis research question (s)
3. identify the theoretical and policy implications of the study with respect to the overall study area
4. highlight the study limitations
5. provide direction and areas for future research

Almost like a thesis on the study, it should have a beginning (introduction), a middle section (synthesis of empirical findings as answers to research questions), theoretical and policy implications and an end (future direction and direction of further research).

2.7 Empirical Findings

The discussion under this section should provide a synthesis of the empirical findings from the study with respect to the individual research questions. Provide evidence and synthesis of arguments presented in the body to show how these converge to answer the research question, and or study objectives. Don't summarize! This can be done by including a brief summary of the main finding in the different chapters that these points seek to provide answers to or the specific research question being addressed in the conclusion. It is bad to simply repeat earlier arguments that were in your thesis. Instead, show your reader how the points you made and the support and examples you used fit together. Pull it all together for them. Do this systematically for all the different research questions of the thesis. Then, you may give a brief summary of your argument and identify the main reasons/causes/factors that relate to the questions you have. If there are two or more parts to the question, be sure to include responses to each part in your conclusion.

2.7.1 Theoretical Implication

In this section you attempt to briefly argue how your findings could influence further understanding or application knowledge in the subject. Whilst you should not attempt to underestimate existing positions and views on such subjects, it is critical that you present a modest position of how your work has contributed to existing understanding of concepts that have been investigated by the project. In cases where your findings differ from those of others, it is useful to indicate possible reasons for such variation. Moreover, it is equally important to acknowledge the views of others who share similar positions as those identified by your research. In a nut shell, show how your finding differ or support those of others and why.

2.7.2 Policy implication

Here, you mention the main theoretical understanding on which your research has been based. It would be appropriate to posit how your findings may affect practice in that field of study in future.

2.8 Recommendation for future research

When discussing the need for future research:

- Outline your plans regarding further research of the topic or aspects of the project that have not been covered in the present study but are considerably worthwhile to investigate in the near future.
- You can provide such an outline in bullet points and provide a brief explanation for each of the research statements.
- Keep this simple and short.

2.9 Conclusion section of the conclusion chapter

Finally, it is a good idea to add a sentence or two to reinforce the thesis statement which was used in your introduction. This shows the reader that you have done what you said you would do and gives a sense of unity to the thesis.

Make sure your chapter has an ending. The final two or three paragraphs are as important as any other paragraph. You could talk about the overall significance of the study, the subject in general, and how it is important to know about it, how it can contribute to "the body of knowledge with the areas of study ", or maybe world view. Make the reader feel that it has been worth his or her while to read the thesis and that the area of study has advanced with your work.

It is important to end the conclusion chapter (in the case of thesis) with a very short paragraph as a conclusion. This section serves as the capsule for the overall conclusion of the study and should therefore be very concise and precise.

2.10 Recommendations

Recommendations must be drawn from the findings and the conclusions and follow the SMART principle: S for specific, M for measurable, A for Action-oriented, R for realistic and T for time-bound. Recommendations may be in the form of policy, action measures and suggested areas for further research.

CHAPTER THREE
REFERENCES AND APPENDICES

3.1 Bibliographic References and Appendices

After writing the first three chapters of the proposal go to bibliography. Your proposal should contain a working bibliography of key texts that inform your study and methodology. You should include all sources cited in your proposal.

This section contains the listing of the materials read by the researcher or used in the study. The bibliography follows the American Psychological Association or APA style.

Examples of the APA format are shown below:

3.1.1 Citations

APA Style uses brief citations within the text of a paper when referring to a source. The brief citation gives the author(s) and year of the source in parentheses, allowing readers to locate the full citation in your reference list at the end of your paper.

Examples:

-Early onset results were reported in a more persistent and severe course (Kessler, 2003).

-Kessler (2003) found that early onset results in a more persistent and severe course.

-When reproducing a direct quote, include the specific page number(s). You are encouraged to include page numbers when paraphrasing.

Examples:

Svanum and Aigner (2011) found "students who did well were prone to view the course more positively" (p. 676).

"Students who did well were prone to view the course more positively" (Svanum & Aigner, 2011, p.676)

No page numbers?

Many online sources do not have page numbers. For direct quotes, use a paragraph number, or cite the heading and the number of paragraphs following it.
Examples:
(Basu & Jones, 2007, para. 4)
(Verbunt, Pernot, & Smeets, 2008, Discussion section, para. 1)

No author?

Use the first few words of the title instead. Within parentheses, use quotation marks around the title of an article, a chapter, or a web page; Italicize the name of a journal, newspaper, magazine, or book.
Examples:
("Study Finds", 2007)
(*College Bound Seniors*, 2008, pp. 42-3)
For more information on citing sources within your paper, see pp. 174-79 of the *Publication Manual of the American Psychological Association*, 6th edition.

3.1.2 Citation (Quotations and Summary/Paraphrasing)

Either you are making **a direct reference (quoting)** or you're making an **indirect reference (reporting)** and put it in your own morphological clothing. In both cases you are required to remain loyal to the works of others.

When you refer to the works of others, you're connecting your own work to the works of others. Since we're making claims in our studies and these claims have to be supported; one way of supporting our claims is referring to the works of others and use the ideas that have been developed by others. Through citation, you adhere to works of others and place yourself in a particular community. This way, you do a number of things:
1- getting membership to a particular community.
2- getting acceptance from readers

3.1.3 Quotations
Short Quotations

When you **directly quote** 40 words or fewer from a work, you need to include **the author, year of publication, and the page number** for the reference (preceded by "p."). Introduce the quotation with a signal phrase that includes the author's last name followed by the date of publication in parentheses.
According to Jones (1998), "Students often had difficulty using APA style, especially when it was their first time" (p. 199).
Jones (1998) found "students often had difficulty using APA style" (p. 199); what implications does this have for teachers?

If the author is not named in a signal phrase, place the author's last name, the year of publication, and the page number in parentheses after the quotation.

She stated, "Students often had difficulty using APA style" (Jones, 1998, p. 199), but she did not offer an explanation as to why.

Long quotations

Place direct quotations that **are 40 words, or longer**, in a free-standing block of typewritten lines, and omit quotation marks. Start the quotation on a new line, indented 1/2 inch from the left margin, i.e., in the same place you would begin a new paragraph. **Type the entire quotation on the new margin, and indent the first line of any subsequent paragraph within the quotation 1/2 inch from the new margin**. Maintain double-spacing throughout. The parenthetical citation should come after the closing punctuation mark.

Jones's (1998) study found the following:

Students often had difficulty using APA style, especially when it was their first time citing sources. This difficulty could be attributed to the fact that many students failed to purchase a style manual or to ask their teacher for help. (p. 199)

Summary or paraphrase

If you are reporting (paraphrasing) an idea from another work, you only have to make reference to the author and year of publication in your in-text reference, but APA guidelines encourage you to also provide the page number (although it is not required.) According to Jones (1998), APA style is a difficult citation format for first-time learners.

APA style is a difficult citation format for first-time learners (Jones, 1998, p. 199).

In-Text Citation

When using APA format, follow the author-date method of in-text citation. This means that the author's last name and the year of publication for the source should appear in the text, for example, (Jones, 1998), and a complete reference should appear in the reference list at the end of the paper.

If you are referring to an idea from another work but **NOT** directly quoting the material, or making reference to an entire book, article or other work, you only have to make reference to the author and year of publication and not the page number in your in-text reference. All sources that are cited in the text must appear in the reference list at the end of the paper.

 Note: APA style requires authors to use the past tense or present perfect tense when using signal phrases to describe earlier research, for example, Jones (1998) **found** or Jones (1998) **has found**...

Citing an Author or Authors

A Work by Two Authors: Name both authors in the signal phrase or in the parentheses each time you cite the work. Use the word "and" between the authors' names within the text and use the ampersand in the parentheses.

Research by Wegener and Petty (1994) supports...

(Wegener & Petty, 1994)

A Work by Three to Five Authors: List all the authors in the signal phrase or in parentheses the first time you cite the source.

(Kernis, Cornell, Sun, Berry, & Harlow, 1993)

In subsequent citations, only use the first author's last name followed by "et al." in the signal phrase or in parentheses.

(Kernis et al., 1993)

Note: In *et al.*, *et* should not be followed by a period.

Six or More Authors: Use the first author's name followed by et al. in the signal phrase or in parentheses.

Harris et al. (2001) argued...

(Harris et al., 2001)

Unknown Author: cite the source by its title in the signal phrase or use the first word or two in the parentheses. Titles of books and reports are italicized or underlined; titles of articles, chapters, and web pages are in quotation marks.

A similar study was done of students learning to format research papers ("Using APA," 2001).

Organization as an Author: If the author is an organization or a government agency, mention the organization in the signal phrase or in the parenthetical citation the first time you cite the source.

According to the American Psychological Association (2000), ...

If the organization has a well-known abbreviation, include the abbreviation in brackets the first time the source is cited and then use only the abbreviation in later citations.

First citation: (Mothers Against Drunk Driving [MADD], 2000)
Second citation: (MADD, 2000)

Two or More Works in the Same Parentheses: When your parenthetical citation includes two or more works, order them the same way they appear in the reference list, separated by a semi-colon.

(Berndt, 2002; Harlow, 1983)

Authors with the Same Last Name: To prevent confusion, use first initials with the last names.

(E. Johnson, 2001; L. Johnson, 1998)

Two or More Works by the Same Author in the Same Year: If you have two sources by the same author in the same year, use lower-case letters (a, b, c) with the year to order the entries in the reference list. Use the lower-case letters with the year in the in-text citation.

Research by Berndt (1981a) illustrated that...

Introductions, Prefaces, Forewords, and Afterwords: When citing an Introduction, Preface, Foreword, or Afterwords in-text, cite the appropriate author and year as usual.

(Funk & Kolln, 1992)

Personal Communication: For interviews, letters, e-mails, and other person-to-person communication, cite the communicator's name, the fact that it was personal communication, and the date of the communication. Do not include personal communication in the reference list.

(E. Robbins, personal communication, January 4, 2001).

A. P. Smith also claimed that many of her students had difficulties with APA style (personal communication, November 3, 2002).

Citing Indirect Sources

If you use a source that was cited in another source, name the original source in your signal phrase. List the secondary source in your reference list and include the secondary source in the parentheses.

Johnson argued that...(as cited in Smith, 2003, p. 102).

Electronic Sources

If possible, cite an electronic document the same as any other document by using the author-date style.

Kenneth (2000) explained...

Unknown Author and Unknown Date: If no author or date is given, use the title in your signal phrase and use the abbreviation "n.d." (for "no date").

Another study of students and research decisions discovered that students succeeded with tutoring ("Tutoring and APA," n.d.).

Sources without Page Numbers

When an electronic source lacks page numbers, you should try to include information that will help readers find the passage being cited. When an electronic document has numbered paragraphs, use the abbreviation "para." followed by the paragraph number (Hall, 2001, para. 5). If the paragraphs are not numbered and the document includes headings, provide the appropriate heading and specify the paragraph under that heading. Note that in some electronic sources, like Web pages, people can use the Find function in their browser to locate any passages you cite.

According to Smith (1997), ... (Mind over Matter section, para. 6).

Note: Never use the page numbers of Web pages you print out; different computers print Web pages with different pagination.

3.2 Reference List (Bibliography)

The following are examples of the most commonly used sources. For examples not given here, refer to the *Publication Manual of the American Psychological Association*.

Capitalization: In your reference list, only capitalize the first letter of all words in periodical titles. For other titles (i.e. books, articles, or Web pages) capitalize only the first letter of the first word of the title and subtitle, and proper nouns.

ARTICLES

Journal Article (print):

For articles with up to and including 7 authors*, include the names of all authors.

Author, A. A., & Author, B. B. (Year). Title of article. *Title of Journal, volume number*(issue number), pages.

Kozma, A., & Stones, M. J. (1983). Re-validation of the Memorial University of Newfoundland scale of happiness.
Canadian Journal on Aging, 2(1), 27-29.

Journal Article (8 or more authors):

Use ellipses after the name of the sixth author, and then list the last author named.

Gilbert, D. G., McClernon, J. F., Rabinovich, N. E., Sugai, C., Plath, L. C., Asgaard, G., . . . Botros, N. (2004).
Effects of quitting smoking on EEG activation and attention last for more than 31 days and are more severe with stress, dependence, DRD2 A1 allele, and depressive traits. *Nicotine and Tobacco Research, 6,* 249-67.

Journal Article (online):

Provide the doi number (Digital Object Identifier).

Author, A. A. (Year). Title of article. *Title of Journal, volume number*(issue number), pages. doi:xxxxxxxxxxxxxxxx

Fuller, D. (2002). Critical friendships: Reading women's writing communities in Newfoundland. *Women's Studies International Forum, 25*(2), 247-260. doi:10.1016/S0277-5395(02)00234-0

Journal Article (online, no doi):

Provide URL of journal's homepage only if doi is not available. Do not include Article Index information.

Author, A. A. (Year). Title of article. *Title of Journal, volume number*(issue number), pages. Retrieved from
   http://journal homepage address

Martin, R. (2001). Educational psychology in Newfoundland and Labrador: A thirty-year history. *Canadian Journal of*
 School Psychology, 16(2), 5-17. Retrieved from: http://cjs.sagepub.com/ Day, Month/ Year. Day, Month/ Year.

Magazine Article (online, no doi):

Provide URL of magazine's homepage only if doi is not available. Omit page numbers for online magazine articles.

Author, A. A. (Year, Month day). Title of article. *Title of Magazine.* Retrieved from http://magazine homepage address Day, Month/ Year.

Capps, R. (2012, October 19). Why things fail: From tires to helicopter blades, everything breaks eventually. *Wired.* Retrieved from http://www.wired.com/ Day, Month/ Year.

Newspaper Article (print):

When referencing a newspaper article, p. (single page) or pp. (multiple pages) precedes the page numbers.

Author, A. A. (Year, Month day). Title of article. *Title of Newspaper,* p. page number(s).

Sullivan, D. D. (2000, November 15). Teens say they're battling depression, peer pressure: 'You kind of drift apart from your parents,' one high school student says. *The Telegram,* p. 17.

Newspaper Article (online, no doi):

Provide URL of newspaper's homepage only if doi is not available. Omit page numbers for online newspaper articles.

Author, A. A. (Year, Month day). Title of article. *Title of Newspaper.* Retrieved from http://newspaper homepage address Day, Month/ Year.

Hurley, C. (2009, October 24). Suzuki encourages Newfoundlanders to join the world in demonstration on climate change. *The Western Star*. Retrieved from http://www.thewesternstar.com/ Day, Month/ Year.

BOOKS

Author, A. A. (Year). *Title of book*. Location: Publisher.

For location, give city name & and state/province abbreviation. Outside North America, spell out city & country names.

Grenfell, W. T. (1919). *A Labrador doctor: The autobiography of Wilfred Thomason Grenfell*. Boston, MA: Houghton

 Mifflin Company.

E-Books

Provide the doi number (Digital Object Identifier) or a URL. Only use a URL if the doi is not available.

Author, A. A. (Year). *Title of book*. doi:xxxxxxxxxxxxxxxx

Moorcroft, W. H. (2005). *Understanding sleep and dreaming*. doi:10.1007/0-387-28698-5

Author, A. A. (Year). *Title of book*. Retrieved from http://URL

Holland, N. N. (1982). *Laughing: A psychology of humor*. Retrieved Day, Month, Year from http://www.uflib.ufl.edu/ufdc/UFDC.aspx?n=palmm&c=psa1&m=hd2J&i=45367

Edited Book

State the editor(s) instead of author, followed by (Ed.) or, for multiple editors (Eds.).

Wright, M. J., & Myers, C. R. (Eds.). (1983). *History of academic psychology in Canada*. Toronto, Canada: Hogrefe and Huber.

Article in an Edited Book

Article Author. (Year). Title of article. In Editor's name (Ed.), *Title of book* (pp. page numbers). Location: Publisher.

Einar, V. K. (2007). Screening of eating disorders in the general population. In P. M. Goldfarb (Ed.), *Psychological*

tests and testing research trends (pp. 141-50). New York, NY: Nova Science.

Edition of a Book, other than the 1st

Author, A. A. (Year). Title of book (x ed.). Location: Publisher.

American Psychiatric Association. (1994). *Diagnostic and statistical manual of mental disorders: DSM-IV* (4th ed.). Washington, DC: Author.

Volume of a Book

If it is an edition other than the 1st, include the edition immediately before the volume number.

Author, A. A. (Year). *Title of book* (x ed., Vol. x). Location: Publisher.

Eisenberg, N. (Ed.). (2006). *Handbook of child psychology* (6th ed., Vol. 3). Hoboken, NJ: John Wiley & Sons.

Translated Book

Author, A. A. (Year). *Title of book*. (A.A. Translator, Trans.). Location: Publisher. (Original work published xxxx).

Freud, S. (1960). *Jokes and their relation to the unconscious*. (J. Strachey, Trans.). London, England: Rutledge & K. Paul. (Original work published 1905).

WEBSITES

If no author is available, begin entry with the title. If no publication date is available, use (n.d.) for "no date".

Author, A. A. (Year, Month day). Title of web page/document. Retrieved from http://URL to specific page

Rose, C. (2012, November 12). How to write citations and bibliographies in APA style. Retrieved Day, Month, Year from http://www.library.mun.ca/guides/howto/apa.php

Newfoundland and Labrador Environment Network. (2011, October 7). Voting for the environment: Environment Network releases review of party policies. Retrieved Day, Month, Year from http://www.nlen.ca/issues/forests/voting-for-the environment-environment-network-releases -review-of-party-policies/

Newfoundland government rejects environmental impact statement for nickel plant. (2008, November 28). Retrieved Day, Month, Year from http://www.miningwatch.ca/newfoundland-government-rejects-environmental-impact-statement-nickel-plant-0

OTHER

Class Lecture:

Instructor, I. I. (Year, Month day). *Title of lecture*. Class lecture for course, University, Location.

Buckle, J. (2011, October 7). *Bereavement*. Class lecture for PSYC 3040: Contemporary issues in death and dying,

Grenfell Campus, Memorial University of Newfoundland, Corner Brook, NL.

Class Notes on Course Website (D2L or My Grenfell):

Provide the file format in brackets after the title (e.g. PDF, PowerPoint slides, Word document).

Instructor, I. I. (Year, Month day). Title [File type]. Retrieved Day, Month, Year from: URL

Fowler, K. (2010, September 20). Memory and cognition [PDF]. Retrieved Day, Month, Year from

http://online.mun.ca/psyc2520%20kfowler/Sept%2020%202010.pdf

Dwyer, S. C. (2011, February 4). PSYC 1001: Introduction to psychology [PowerPoint slides]. Retrieved Day, Month, Year from

https://my.swgc.ca/psyc1001/Feb%204%202011.pptx

Coursepack:

Instructor, I. I. (Year). *Title of coursepack.* Coursepack, University, Location.

Warren, K. (2012). *PSYC 2025: Survey of developmental psychology.* Course pack, Grenfell Campus, Memorial University of Newfoundland, Corner Brook, NL.

Dictionary/Encyclopedia (Print):

Author, A. A. (if available). (Year). Title of entry. In B. B. Editor (Ed.), *Title of dictionary/encyclopedia* (p. page number).

Location: Publisher.

Facial expression. (2007). In G.R. VandenBos (Ed.), *APA dictionary of psychology* (pp. 362-3). Washington, DC:

American Psychological Association.

Dictionary/Encyclopedia (Online):

Provide the doi number (Digital Object Identifier) or a URL. Only use a URL if the doi is not available. If there are no page numbers, the entry title is sufficient.

Author, A. A. (if available). (Year). Title of entry. In B.B. Editor (Ed.), *Title of dictionary/encyclopedia.* (p. page number).doi:xxxxxxxxxxxxxxxx OR Retrieved from http://URL

Roesch, S. (2006). Coping mechanisms. In Y. K. Jackson (Ed.), *Encyclopedia of multicultural psychology.* Retrieved from http://www.sage-ereference.com.qe2a-proxy.mun.ca/multiculturalpsychology/Article_n53.html

Dissertation or Thesis (Print):

Author, A. A. (Year). *Title of dissertation/thesis* (Doctoral dissertation OR master's thesis). University, Location.

Broderick, E. M. (2007). *Assessment of grief and loss services in western Newfoundland* (Honours dissertation).

Grenfell Campus, Memorial University of Newfoundland, Corner Brook, NL.

Dissertation or Thesis (Online):

If accessed through an Article Index, include the name of the database, and give the accession or order number in parentheses at the end of the entry. If accessed on the internet, include the URL link.

Author, A. A. (Year). *Title of dissertation/ thesis* (Doctoral dissertation OR master's thesis). Available from Name of Database. (accession or order number)

Rusch, L. C. (2010). *Depression stigma reduction: The impact of models of depression on stigma and treatment seeking*

(Doctoral dissertation). Available from ProQuest dissertation and theses database. (Document ID 1865749061)

Government Document, Canadian (Print):

Only indicate jurisdiction (i.e. Country, Province, or City) if it's not apparent elsewhere in the citation. If the author is also the publisher, use "Author" to indicate publisher.

Jurisdiction.GovernmentDepartment/Organization/Committee. (Year, Month day). *Title of document or report* (Report no. xxx).Location, Publisher.

Newfoundland and Labrador. Community Services Council. (2008). *Research papers on people, partners, and prosperity: A strategic plan for Newfoundland and Labrador.* St. John's, NL: Author.

Canadian Institute for Health Information. (2012). *Regulated nurses: Canadian trends, 2006 to 2010.* Ottawa, ON: Author.

Government Document, Canadian (Internet):

"For documents retrieved online, identify the publisher as part of the retrieval statement unless the publisher has been identified as the author" (section 7.03).

Center for Science in the Earth System. (2007, September). *Preparing for climate change: A guidebook for local, regional, and state governments.* Retrieved from Newfoundland and Labrador Environment and Conservation website: http://www.env.gov.nl.ca/env/climate_change/adapting/king_county_guidebook.pdf Newfoundland and Labrador. Health and Community Services. (2005, November). *Newfoundland and Labrador gambling prevalence study.* Retrieved from http://www.health.gov.nl.ca/health/publications/ gambling_report_nov21.pdf

Interview:

Personal communications (e.g. interviews, letters, emails) are not included in the reference list. Cite in-text only.

(J. A. Smith, personal communication, May 29, 2005)

Movie:

Producer, A. A. & Director, B. B. (Year). *Title of motion picture* [Motion picture]. Country of origin: Studio.

Bender, L., Burns, S. Z., & David, L. (Producers), & Guggenheim, D. (Director). (2006). *An inconvenient truth* [Motion picture].United States: Paramount.

3.3 Appendices

Materials that are pertinent to the research but may distort the logical flow of the paper should be placed at the back. Each appendix must be properly numbered and paginated.

If a survey will be conducted, the research instrument will have to be attached to the thesis or dissertation proposal as part of the appendix including a cover letter.

CHAPTER FOUR
THE FINAL RESEARCH PAPER

4.1 The Final Research Paper
4.1.1 General Requirements

A thesis or dissertation must (except for the list of abbreviations) contain as part of the preliminaries, a title page, a certificate of originality, an approval sheet, an acknowledgement page, an abstract, a table of contents, a list of tables, a list of figures, and a list of abbreviated entries or acronyms (which is optional). A thesis or dissertation must follow the prescribed format and should be typed in Times New Roman, font 12. Except for the title page, all pages should have a two- inch margin on the left and one – inch margin on the right side.

Paper, Spacing, Margins, Font Size, Pagination and Length of the Research Proposal

The proposal as well as final copy of the thesis / dissertation must be written on a 8.5*11 inches, 20-pound white bond paper with a 25% or higher rag content (watermark should be visible).

All copies must be free of smudges and blemishes. Typing of the manuscript is only one side of the paper. As to spacing, the text is double- spaced throughout. However, single spacing is used for blocked quotations on the text as well as for footnotes and bibliographic items but double spaced between such items.

Triple – or quadruple- spacing is also allowed after chapter titles, before major subheading, and before and after tables in the text, as this can improve appearance and readability.

In the case of margins, the following must be used:

2 inches left side, 1 inch right side

1 inch top and bottom margins

1 inch above a chapter number

Double space between a chapter number and a title

Quadruple space below a chapter title
Triple space above and below a centered heading
Triple space above a side heading
Double space below a side heading

4.1.2 Font style and size

As a common standard, Times New Roman will be used with font size at 12.

Pages in the preliminaries use lower case roman numerals, while throughout the manuscript, Arabic numerals will be used. All pages must be paginated including the appendices. The pages, except for the first page of each chapter, are numbered at the right hand side about $^3/_4$inch below the top edge and 1 inch from the right side of the page.

In the case of length of the thesis or dissertation proposal or its final version, there is no prescribed length, as this is based on content.

4.2 The Final Paper Oral Defense
4.2.1 Scheduling of the Thesis or Dissertation Oral Defense

Once there are already written endorsements of the thesis or dissertation adviser and the Critic/Reader that a thesis or dissertation has satisfied the standards of thesis or dissertation writing and that of the Graduate School, the draft will now be distributed to the chair and the members of the thesis or dissertation panel.

Copies of the thesis, or dissertation in loose pages(not bound) should be submitted to the Dean's office with the endorsement of the Adviser, at least seven working days before the scheduled oral defense. If there are deficiencies in the thesis or dissertation, the members are given five working days to propose deferment of the oral defense.

Rules Governing the Thesis or Dissertation Oral Defense

The candidate, the adviser and the members of the panel will be informed of the date of the oral defense at least one week before the oral defense. Thus, the panel chair and members are expected to have read the thesis or dissertation prior to the oral defense and as such, formulated their questions and must be ready to offer specific suggestions with regard to the questions that they ask.

4.2.2 The Oral Defense Procedure -The Panel Chair will remind the candidate as to the Considerations for Grading, which are as follows:

- Content, which is rated 30%, refers to the thesis or dissertation manuscript itself. The focus shall be on the substance rather than the format and the style.

- Presentation, which is rated 30%), refers to the way the candidate presents 'and elaborates on the content of the paper in an organized and logical manner. Focus will be on the candidate's mastery of the thesis or dissertation.

Defense, which is rated 40% focuses on the ability of the candidate to satisfactorily answer the questions raised by the panel.

4.3 Ethics in Research
4.3.1 Academic Honesty

The integrity of scholarship is the cornerstone of the academic and social structure of the University. Every aspect of graduate academic life shall be conducted in an absolutely and uncompromisingly honest manner. Hence the Graduate school shall ensure the integrity of all researches conducted and will respond to any allegation of research misconduct in a thorough, competent, timely, objective, and fair manner. Research misconduct is defined as fabrication, falsification, or plagiarism in proposing, performing, or reviewing research, or in reporting research results.

Students who are accused of misconduct related to research will be a reason for getting a failing grade in the oral defense and will be dealt with in accordance with the rules and procedures governing student disciplinary cases in the University.

4.3.2 Research involving Human or Animal subjects

All research involving human or animal subjects requires prior ethical review and approval by an independent review committee composed of the Adviser, program coordinator and the Dean. No data or recruitment of subjects may take place without such approval.

Before beginning a research study, the student should consult with his adviser regarding the procedure for obtaining appropriate ethical review. Copies of the necessary forms and instructions for submission can be obtained from the Office of the Dean.

In cases where research involving human or animal subjects is being performed at another institution, approval also must be obtained from that institution's review committee (s). Copies of such approval should be attached to the proposal to expedite the review process.

4.4 Length, Style, Visual Aids, and Voice
A. Length

Proposals are usually about 20 pages. Conciseness is usually at a premium. The tight focus you have developed on your research problem should, in turn, focus the amount of time and space you spend reviewing relevant literature and discussing methods. Some supervisors may require a more in-depth proposal, from 30-40 pages in length. In some fields the proposal is the first three chapters of a thesis (introduction, methodology, review of literature).

B. Style Considerations
Tone

Tone is the writers' attitude toward their writing, generally expressed most clearly in vocabulary choices and "hedging" considerations.

- Have a consistently confident tone.
- Don't use an apologetic or arrogant tone.

Coherence

Coherence is the extent to which sentences and paragraphs "flow" together. It allows your readers to follow your writing. Usually, when readers say something "logically fits," they mean that it is coherent. Writers can achieve coherence by

- Moving from **"old"** (familiar) information to **"new"** information.
- Putting more important information at the end of the sentence (stress position).
- Keeping the subject and verb together.
- Starting sentences with **short, easily understood phrases**.
- Using **"stock" transitional phrases** ("however," "therefore," "in addition," "on the other hand") that signal to readers a shift in topic or emphasis.
- Using **pronouns** to refer back to previously introduced information (e.g. this+noun) and/or the use of **recycling**, or the repetition of key words or phrases.

C. Voice

Voice is your "presence" as a grammatical subject in your sentences. Be conscious of the difference between "active" and "passive" voice.

D. Visual Aids

Include graphs, charts, illustrations, diagrams, etc., wherever permissible, possible, or practical.

CHAPTER FIVE

A Sample Proposal

University of xxxxx
MA Proposal of English Language Teaching

Subject:

The effect of using translation from L1 to L2 as a teaching technique in the improvement of Iranian EFL learners' linguistic accuracy— focus on form

Proposal Advisor:
Xxxx xxx, PhD

Consulting advisor:
Xxxxx xxxxx, PhD

By:
Xxxx xxxxx
2006-2007

1. Introduction

The debate over whether English language classrooms should include or exclude students' native language has been a contentious issue for a long time (Brown, 2000, p. 195). Although the use of mother tongue has been banned since the emergence of Direct Method, there are still figures who advocate the use of L1 in the classroom. According to Cook (2001) "bringing the L1 back from exile may lead not only to the improvement of existing teaching methods but also to innovations in methodology. In particular, it may liberate the task-based learning approach so that it can foster the students' natural collaborative efforts in the classroom through their L1 as well as their L2" (p. 189).

Dörnyei and Kormos (1998) found that the L1 is used by L2 learners as a communication strategy to compensate for deficiencies in the target language. Auerbuch (1993) not only acknowledges the positive role of the mother tongue in the classroom, but also identifies the following uses for it: classroom management, language analysis and presenting rules that govern grammar, discussing cross-cultural issues, giving instructions or prompts, explaining errors, and checking for comprehension.

Obviously, one of the noticeable aspects of L1 use is translation which can serve as a teaching technique. Cook (2001) asserts that the word 'translation' has so far been avoided as much as possible because of its negative implication in teaching. "Translation as a *teaching technique* is a different matter from translation as a goal of language teaching" (p. 200).

On the other hand, focus on form, in its communicative sense, is defined by Richards and Schmidt (2002) as any focusing of attention on the formal linguistic characteristics of language, as opposed to a pure focus on meaning in communication. In a more technical sense, focus on form has been defined as "a brief allocation of attention to linguistic form as the need for this arises incidentally, in the context of communication" (p. 205). The significance of focus on form has been well appreciated by Ellis (2002) who claims that "there is by now ample evidence to show that form-focused instruction (FFI) has a positive effect on second language (SL) acquisition. That is, by and large, learners seem to learn the grammatical structures they are taught" (p. 225).

Similarly, this research study tries to utilize an instrument which would lead to the reinforcement of focus on form whose chief object is to enhance linguistic accuracy. The instrument which is used in this study for such a purpose is translation from L1 to L2. The idea of using translation as a teaching method has also been supported in the literature. Duff (1989) states that "translation does not have to be a lone, pointless struggle between student and text. Many other approaches are possible. Translation can be introduced purposefully and imaginatively, into the language learning program. If we can find a way to offset the weak points and make the best use of its assets, translation as a teaching technique can be used to help students learn a second language more thoughtfully and effectively" (p. 6).

1.1. Statement of the Problem

This study is an attempt to examine whether using translation from L1 to L2 has any effect in the improvement of a group of Iranian EFL learners' linguistic accuracy—focus on form—or not.

1.2. Research Question

The research question formulated for the purpose of this study is as follows:

Does the use of translation from L1 to L2 have any effect in the improvement of Iranian EFL learners' linguistic accuracy—focus on form?

1.3. Statement of Hypothesis

The null hypothesis of the present study is:

Using translation from L1 to L2 has no effect on the improvement of Iranian EFL learners' linguistic accuracy—focus on form.

1.4. Significance of the Study

The significance of this study is appreciated from two respects. Firstly, this study signifies the role that mother tongue can play in second language learning. In effect, although the use of learners' first language has been banned since the immergence of Direct Method at the end of the nineteenth century (Cook, 2001), it has recurrently been noted that mother tongue is a rich resource which can help one to improve his/her second language learning. "While the English Only paradigm continues to be dominant in communicative ELT, research into teacher practice reveals that the L1 is used as a learning resource in many ESL classes" (Auerbach, 1993, p. 15). Therefore, translation, as an obvious feature of L1 use, is used in this study to lay emphasis on the focus on form whose chief goal is to enhance linguistic accuracy.

Secondly, another feature of communicative language teaching, which is nowadays widely used, is the fact that in CLT gives more prominence to fluency than accuracy. As a result of this mere focus on meaning and deemphasizing accuracy in CLT classes, the present study aims at using a teaching technique to improve linguistic accuracy-- focus on form-- of Iranian EFL learners. In other words, this study tries to investigate the efficiency of a teaching technique— namely translating from L1 to L2—in enhancing Iranian intermediate learners' focus on form by means of using particular grammatical structures. As Duff (1989) puts it, "translation as a teaching technique can be used to help students learn a second language more thoughtfully and effectively" (p. 6). Although focus on form can be achieved through different techniques, the present study aims at introducing an alternative technique-- translation from L1 to L2-- to reach the same goal.

In fact, the idea of this research has been primarily inspired by the contribution of both the researcher's area of interest and the learners' feedback after experiencing this technique. In other words, the mentioned technique has been employed in the researcher's own classes and, surprisingly, it has gained favor with the learners in most cases. Receiving such a positive feedback from the learners in this respect was a strong motivation for carrying out this study.

1.5. Definition of Key Terms

Explicit focus on form: Explicit focus on form refers to the time when an error is explicitly referred to, and the learner is directly told that *it is not X but it is Y*. This kind of focus on form could be done through explicit or direct strategies which again involve explicitly drawing the attention of learners to the error with or without rule explanation. Further, Doughty and Williams (1998) state that explicit focus on form "is to *direct* learners' attention to *exploit pedagogical the grammar* in this regard" (p. 232).

Focus on form: Focus on form has been defined as "a brief allocation of attention to linguistic form as the need for this arises incidentally, in the context of communication" (Richards and Schmidt, 2002, p. 205). Moreover, focus on form, in contrast to focus on formS, "consists of an occasional shift of attention to linguistic code features—by the teacher and/ or one or more students—triggered by perceived problems with comprehension or production" (Long& Robbins, 1998, p. 23).

Translation: The process of rendering written language that was produced in one language (the source language) into another (the target language), or the target language version that results from this process.

2. Review of Related Literature
2.1. Introduction

In this chapter, some key issues related to the justification of using the mother tongue in EFL classrooms, the significance of using translation as a teaching technique in teaching a foreign language, and the importance and aspects of focus on form in EFL contexts will be elaborated on.

2.2. The Role of Mother Tongue in Second Language Learning

The debate over whether English language classrooms should include or exclude students' native language has been a contentious issue for a long time (Brown, 2000, p. 195). Although the use of mother tongue has been banned since the emergence of Direct Method, there are still figures who advocate the use of L1 in the classroom. According to Cook (2001) "bringing the L1 back from exile may lead not only to the improvement of existing teaching methods but also to innovations in methodology. In particular, it may liberate the task-based learning approach so that it can foster the students' natural collaborative efforts in the classroom through their L1 as well as their L2" (p. 189).

Dörnyei and Kormos (1998) find that the L1 is used by L2 learners as a communication strategy to compensate for deficiencies in the target language. Auerbuch (1993) not only acknowledges the positive role of the mother tongue in the classroom, but also identifies the following uses for it: classroom management, language analysis and presenting rules that govern grammar, discussing cross-cultural issues, giving instructions or prompts, explaining errors, and checking for comprehension. Furthermore, "when the native language *is* used, practitioners, researchers, and learners consistently report positive results" (Auerbach, 1993, p. 18).

Moreover, Cook (1999) claims that "treating the L1 as a classroom resource opens up several ways to use it, such as for teachers to convey meaning, explain grammar, and organize the class, and for students to use as part of their collaborative learning and individual strategy use. The first language can be a useful element in creating authentic L2 users rather than something to be shunned at all costs" (p. 185).

Although the provision of maximum L2 exposure to the learners seems essential, L1 can be used alongside L2 as a complement. In this regard, Turnbull (2001) states that "for me, maximizing the target language does not and should not mean that it is harmful for the teacher to use the L1. A principle that promotes maximal teacher use of the target language acknowledges that the L1 and target language can exist simultaneously" (p. 153). As Stern (1992, p. 285) suggests, use of L1 and target language should be seen as complementary, depending on the characteristics and stages of the language learning process.

On the other hand, overuse of L1 will naturally reduce the amount of exposure to L2. Therefore, attempt should be made to keep a balance between L1 and L2 use. Turnbull (2001) believes that using the L1 can save time in the EFL/ ESL classroom. He adds that "I agree that it is efficient to make a quick switch to the L1 to ensure that students understand a difficult grammar concept or an unknown word. However, it is crucial for teachers to use the TL as much as possible in contexts in which students spend only short periods of time in class on a daily basis, and when they have little contact with the TL outside the classroom" (p. 160).

2.3. Using Translation as a Teaching Technique in L2 Teaching

Obviously, one of the noticeable aspects of L1 use is translation which can serve as a teaching technique. Also, the idea of using translation as a teaching technique has been supported in the literature. Cook (2001) asserts that the word 'translation' has so far been avoided as much as possible because of its pejorative overtones in teaching. "Translation as a *teaching technique* is a different matter from translation as a goal of language teaching" (p. 200).

Similarly, Duff (1989) states that "translation does not have to be a lone, pointless struggle between student and text. Many other approaches are possible. Translation can be introduced purposefully and imaginatively, into the language learning program. If we can find a way to offset the weak points and make the best use of its assets, translation as a teaching technique can be used to help students learn a second language more thoughtfully and effectively" (p. 6).

A number of scholars view the two extreme positions of pure translation and forbidding translation in the classroom as unnecessary extremes and instead, advocate for a balanced approach in which teachers strategically use L1 in order to promote foreign language acquisition. Stibbard (1994) analyzed the use of oral translation as a L2 teaching activity. He suggested that translation may play a valuable role in L2 teaching. Moreover, he asserted that translation should be an integral part of the language-learning program. Levenston (1985) presented an overview of the role of translation in foreign language teaching and learning. He argued that translation is useful for: (1) practicing grammatical structures, (2) explaining vocabulary items, (3) testing at all levels, and (4) developing communicative competence. He recommended translation be taught as a skill in its own right.

According to Chellapan (1982), we should not simply eliminate translation but we should absorb translation into a larger creative process of learning. He points out; "Translation can make the student come to closer grips with the target language. A simultaneous awareness of two media could actually make the student see the points of convergence and divergence more clearly and also refine the tools of perception and analysis resulting in divergent thinking" (p. 60).

A significant benefit of translation in language teaching is that teachers can use translation as an effective means of explaining particular aspects of language, such as cultural differences, grammatical rules and syntactic structures with which the students have difficulty. In this regard, Chellapan (1982) explains that this way of using translation involves a conscious process of learning. Through translation, a learner can be aware of the distinctiveness of similar structures in the two languages, and also of the different processes used in conveying the same message. "Deliberate translation," as he calls it, focuses on lexical items, where the contrasts in the two languages vary, but it should be done in a larger context. This will help the students learn the different distributions in the two languages and also show that the meaning of any item is part of the total environment of the text in the two languages.

Another benefit of using translation is that it helps to develop the learners competence and to improve performance. According to Chomsky (1965), there is a clear distinction between competence (the knowledge of a language) and performance (the actual use of language in a concrete situation). In Chomsky's view, the learners' ability to perform is based on his/her competence, which is entirely linguistic. Hymes (1972), on the contrary, proposes a broader notion of competence, that of communicative competence. He claims that the learners' performance reflects both knowledge of grammatical rules and knowledge of how these rules are used to communicate meaning, knowledge of when, where, and with whom to use the rules.

Hymes stresses that the learners ability to perform needs to be understood in terms of communicative competence rather than linguistic competence.

For translation to be whether linguistic or both linguistic and communicative is not the focus of this study; rather, the main concern is to argue that translation can be used effectively to help learners acquire the most important linguistic ability, that is the ability "to understand and to produce utterances which are grammatical as well as appropriate to the context in which they are made" (Campbell and Wales, 1970, p.247).

As for the students' knowledge of linguistic rules, the translation method can be used very successfully to teach grammar and structural patterns. It helps point out and clarify the differences between the grammatical system and syntactic structures in the target and the native languages. As mentioned, translation, more than other methods of instruction enables students to understand more clearly how various grammatical features are used.

2.4. Focus on Form

Focus on form, in its communicative sense, is defined as any focusing of attention on the formal linguistic characteristics of language, as opposed to a pure focus on meaning in communication. In a more technical sense, focus on form has been defined as "a brief allocation of attention to linguistic form as the need for this arises incidentally, in the context of communication" (Richards and Schmidt, 2002, p. 205). The significance of focus on form has been well appreciated by Ellis (2002) who claims that "there is by now ample evidence to show that form-focused instruction (FFI) has a positive effect on second language (SL) acquisition. That is, by and large, learners seem to learn the grammatical structures they are taught" (p. 225).

In a research to investigate the effect of focus on form on the quality of instruction, M. Lightbown and Spada's (1994) observations of the intensive program classes revealed that overall the instruction focused on meaning-based activities, and teachers gave little attention to grammar or accuracy. Their observations also indicated, however, that some teachers responded to learners' errors more often than others and that, in some cases, this response appeared to be related to the achievement of higher levels of accuracy.

Research into focus on form (Nunan, 1989) and into the practices of good language learners (Naiman, Frohlich, Stern, & Todesco, 1996) reveals the importance of metalinguistic explanation in adult second language learning, particularly when learning involves abstract notions. Some of this explanation, however, must be done in the L1 if it is to be understood by lower level learners.

Norris and Ortega (2000) in a meta-analysis of 49 Focus on Form Instruction studies found that not only did focus on form make a difference but also that it made a very considerable difference. Their analysis also found that explicit instruction was significantly more effective than implicit instruction and that the effects of focus on form were durable. Moreover, Ellis (2001) claims that "language acquisition can be speeded by explicit instruction" (p. 145).

Ellis (2002) comments that "there is a general agreement and strong empirical evidence to show that focus on form can affect explicit knowledge. It seems reasonable to conclude that it is easier to teach explicit knowledge than implicit knowledge" (p. 234).

Moreover, Robinson and Long (1998) assert that "code switching could also be added to teacher techniques such as recast, which aim at drawing learners' attention to errors performed during communicative activities. The use of L1 could be considered then as a strategy helping to introduce a 'focus on form' in the foreign language classroom" (p. 56).

3. Method

This chapter deals with the different components of the methodology which includes the participants, instrumentation, and procedure.

3.1. Participants

In order to achieve the objectives of this study, 120 participants studying at Paniz Language Institute and City Training Center (Eshragh Branch) and Kish Language Institute will take part in the first phase of the research. The participants are male intermediate learners of English and their age range from 13 to 20 years old. They will be given a test which tests their control over certain structures. Having collected data from this test, 60 of the participants who proved to lack the required knowledge about the intended structures will be selected for the second phase of the study. Then, they will be divided into two groups of 30— one the experimental group, and a control group.

3.2. Instrumentation

In order to carry out the study, a teacher-made achievement test, which comprises the newly introduced structures of *New Interchange 2* course book, is developed in multiple-choice format. In fact, the reason for developing such a test is to make sure that the participants do not have any familiarity with the specific structures under study. It is worth mentioning that three items for each intended structure is used so as to discriminate the participants who have knowledge about the selected structures from those who do not. In other words, those participants who cannot answer any or just one of the items form each intended structure would prove to have lack of control on those specific structures and therefore are suitable for the study.

The instrument used for the treatment is a series of Farsi sentences which are developed in accordance with the structures which have already been taught in each session. The participants have to translate these sentences into English using the specific structure they have learnt in that session.

Finally, another teacher-made achievement test will be used after implementing the treatment to both experimental and control group to find out to what extend the teaching technique used in this study was effective.

3.3. Procedure

This study requires 60 homogeneous learners who also have no familiarity with the following grammatical structures namely **used to do** (along with question and negative forms), **passive voice** (with simple present, present continuous, simple past, past continuous, future with *'going to'* and *'will'*) **conditional type 1 and type 2** and **present**

perfect.

To select such a population, 100 intermediate learners who have not studied *New Interchange 2* course book yet are given a multiple- choice test which includes questions testing the learners' knowledge of the mentioned grammatical structures. There will be 3 items which test each of these structures. The reason for this is to discriminate the participants who have knowledge about the selected structures from those who do not. Consequently, those participants who cannot answer any of the items related to each intended structure or can answer only one of them will be selected for the study. In fact, such a test will help the researcher identify those suitable for the study have no control over those structures which are going to be worked on in the study.

The next step would be to select 60 of the participants who were qualified in the first phase; that is, those who did not have knowledge about the structures to be worked on in the study. These participants will be divided into two groups— one comparison group and the other one the experimental group. The experimental group will receive the treatment in the following way: having taught the new structures— namely *used to do, passive voice, conditional type 1 and type 2* and *present perfect* — in each session, the participants will be given 7 sentences in Persian which are developed in accordance with the structures which have already been taught in that session. The participants have to translate these sentences into English, individually, using the specific structure they have learnt in that session.

The participants should do the task inside the classroom and individually. After that, the teacher will check the participants' answers and correct their linguistic mistakes in terms of *accurate* use of the specific structure under study.

However, the control group will receive the placebo in the form of the exercises available in their course book which are done monolingually. In other words, the placebo will be the tasks and the exercises that the participants perform as directed in the course book.

Having finished teaching all the structures, the final step is to give a post-test to investigate the effectiveness of the teaching technique used for the experimental group. The test will be given to both experimental and control group and the results from both groups will be compared and will show whether this technique was effective in enhancing linguistic accuracy of the experimental group.

REFERENCES

Ary, D., Jacobs, L.C. & Razavieh, A. (2002). *Introduction to research in education* (6th ed.). Orlando, FL: Harccourt Braca College Publishers.

Auerbach, E. (1993). Reexamining English only in the ESL classroom. *TESOL Quarterly 27*, (1), pp. 9–32.

Bagheri,M.S. & Haghighat,Z(2012).A guide to writing proposals, theses, and dissertations. Shiraz: Ide Derakhshan Publications.

Brown, J.D. (1995). *Understanding research methods in applied linguistics*. Tehran: Payame Noor University Press.

Brown, H. (2000). *Principles of language learning and teaching*. Longman: San Francisco

Brown, J.D., & Rodgers, T.S. (2002). *Doing second language research*. Oxford, UK: Oxford University Press.

Campbell, R. & Wales, R. (1970). The study of language acquisition. In John Lyons (Eds.), *New horizons in Linguistics* (pp. 242–293). Harmonswort: Penguin Books.

Chellapan, K. (1982). Translanguage, translation and second language acquisition. In F. Eppert (Eds.), *Papers on translation: Aspects, concepts, implications* (pp. 57–63). Singapore: SEMEO Regional Language Centre.

Chomsky, N. (1965). Aspects of the theory of syntax. Cambridge: M.I.T. Press.

Cook, V.J. (1999). Going beyond the native speaker in language teaching. *TESOL Quarterly, 33*, (2), 185-209.

Cook, V.J. (2001). Using the first language in the classroom. *Canadian Modern Language Review, 57*, (3), 184-206.

Dörnyei, Z. and J. Kormos. 1998. Problem-solving mechanisms in L2 communication: A psycholinguistic perspective. *Studies in Second Language Acquisition, 20*, (3), pp. 349–385.

Dornyei, Z. (2003). *Questionnaires in second language research: Construction, administration, and processing*. New York: Lawrence Erlbaum Associates.

Dornyei, Z. (2008). *Research methods in applied linguistics*. Oxford: Oxford University Press.

Doughty, C., & Williams, J. (1998). Pedagogical choices in focus on form. In C. Doughty, & J. Williams (Eds.), *Focus on form in classroom second language acquisition* (pp. 197-261). Cambridge: Cambridge University press.

Duff, A. (1989). *Translation*. Oxford: Oxford University Press.

Ellis, R. (2001). Investigating form-focused instruction. *Language Learning, 51*(1), 1-46

Ellis, R. (2002). Does the form-focused instruction affect the acquisition of implicit knowledge? *Studies in Second Language acquisition. 24*, (2), 223-36.

Farhady, H (2002). *Research methods in applied linguistics*. *Tehran*: Payame Noor University Press.

Hymes, D. (1972). On communicative competence. In JB Pride & J. Holmes (Eds.), *Sociolinguistics*. Harmondsworth, England: Penguin Books.

Levenston, E. A. (1985). The place of translation in the foreign language classroom. *English Teachers' Journal, (32),* 33–43.

Lightbown, P. & Spada, N. (1994). An Innovative Program for Primary ESL Students in Quebec. *TESOL Quarterly, 28*(3), 563–80.

Long, M. & Robinson, P. (1998). Focus on form: Theory, research, and practice. In C. Doughty, & J. Williams (Eds.), *Focus on form in second language acquisition (pp. 15-41).* Cambridge University Press.

Mousavi, S.A (1997). *A dictionary of language testing.* Tehran: Rahnama Publications Press.

Naiman, N., Frohlich, M., Stern, H., Todesco, A. (1996). *The good language learner.* Clevedon: Multilingual Matters.

Norris, JM, & Ortega, L. (2000). Effectiveness of L2 instruction: A research synthesis and quantitative meta-analysis. *Language Learning, 50,* 417528.

Nunan, D. (1989). *Designing tasks for the communicative classroom.* London: Cambridge University Press.

Publication Manual of the American Psychological Association (3rd Edition).(1991). Washington, DC: American Psychological Association.

Riazi, A.M. (1991). *A dictionary of research methods: Quantitative and qualitative.* Tehran: Rahnama Publications.

Riazi, A. M. (2000). *How to write research propsals.* Tehran Rahnama Publications Press.

Riazi, A. M. (2002). *Writing academic papers in English.* Shiraz: Shiraz University Press.

Richards. J. C, & Schmidt, R., (2002). *Longman dictionary of language teaching and applied linguistics* (2nd ed.). Essex: Longman Group.

Seliger, H. W. & Shohamy, E. (1989). *Second language research methods.* Oxford: Oxford University Press.

Stern, H. H. (1992). *Issues and options in language teaching.* Oxford: Oxford University Press.

Stibbard, R. (1994). The use of translation in foreign language teaching. *Perspectives: Studies in Translatology, (1),* 9-18.

Turnbull, M. (2001). There is a role for the L1 in second and foreign language teaching, but ... *Canadian Modern Language Review, 57,* (4), 150-163

Yamini, M., & Rahimi, M. (2007). *A guide to statistics and SPSS for research in TEFL, linguistics and related disciplines.* Shiraz: Koshamher.

Internet References

https://owl.english.purdue.edu/
http://psychology.about.com/
http://psych.athabascau.ca/
http://www.library.mun.com

www.ingramcontent.com/pod-product-compliance
Lightning Source LLC
Chambersburg PA
CBHW081157090426
42736CB00017B/3369